Human and Holy

AN IRON ROSE SISTER MINISTRIES
SMALL-GROUP BIBLE STUDY

Michelle J. Goff

WestBow
PRESS
A DIVISION OF THOMAS NELSON

WestBow Press books may be ordered through booksellers or by contacting:

WestBow Press
A Division of Thomas Nelson
1663 Liberty Drive
Bloomington, IN 47403
www.westbowpress.com
1-(866) 928-1240

ISBN: 978-1-4908-0151-3 (sc)
ISBN: 978-1-4908-0152-0 (e)

Library of Congress Control Number: 2013912414

Printed in the United States of America.

WestBow Press rev. date: 8/2/2013

DEDICATION

To my family who has always stood by my side and supported me.

To my "Aaron and Hur" friends who have lifted my arms when I couldn't anymore, who have seen me at my most human moments and have walked with me in my longing to be holy. You are invaluable "lifetime" friends and a testimony to what *Iron Rose Sisters* can and should be.

To my *Iron Rose Sisters* – past, present and future all over the world.

ACKNOWLEDGEMENTS

My primary thanks go to God for His infinite provision. Words cannot express the depth of gratitude to my loving, gracious, heavenly Father.

Secondly, the support of family and friends has been infinite. Without them, I would not be who I am, where I am or able to reach you with these messages!

Countless pages could be filled with the names of many loving brothers and sisters in Christ that have been a part of this journey and have helped make *Human AND Holy* possible. Thank you!

Thank you to Libby Isenhower for the cover photo and Greg Douglas for my bio picture.

Thanks to all those who helped test the *Human AND Holy* study materials: Maryellen Anderson, Tonya Brignac, and others of my Twisted Sisters, Robin Gough, the students at the LSU Christian Student Center, and the Brighton *Iron Rose Sister* Group... Your feedback was vital and your participation was inspiring.

And a special thanks to those who assisted in the editing process! My parents, David and Jocelynn Goff, my grandparents, George and Barbara Brown, Vanessa Gilliam, Jennifer (Goff) Sale, Kimberly (Goff) Edwards, Sherry Hubright, Donna Ellis, Christa Duve, Pam LaPorte, Cindee Stockstill, and Katie Forbess. The constant barrage of questions may have tired you, but your continual support and critiques were invaluable!

Finally, a hat's off to the team at *Westbow Press* for their efforts to meet the goals and deadlines to get *Human AND Holy* in your hands as quickly and professionally as possible.

TABLE OF CONTENTS

PREFACE

Early in the process of writing and getting the materials ready for publication, there was a moment of panic that I felt sure would be repeated. It was a familiar feeling from times in the past when I've taken a leap of faith. The panic stems from doubt and uncertainty that I will be able to accomplish what I feel God has called me to do and be for Him.

Who am I to do this? Aren't there others better-equipped to present studies like this? Who will even be interested in purchasing and participating in these studies? Will the studies be "enough"?

The truth is that no, they won't be enough. And I'm not enough – because that's not what it's about. "Greater is He that is in me than He that is in the world" (I John 4:4). "His divine power has given [me] everything [I] need for life and godliness through [my] knowledge of Him who called [me] by his own glory and goodness" (II Peter 1:3).

And in the same way the women were described after leaving the empty tomb, I feel "afraid, yet filled with joy" (Matthew 28:8).

Throughout my fourteen years of ministry experience, I have had the blessing of walking with women of all ages through the trials, challenges, and joys of life. What an honor to have been a part of their journey! While on that journey, we each come to realize that we cannot "go it alone" and that God has provided us a tremendous guide through His Word and an invaluable network of support through His church, not to mention a tangible example through His Son and the blessing of the Holy Spirit who brings it all together and fills us with His Presence!

It is that blend and balance of emphasis on the Word and on Christian relationships that has always driven me in my quest for women's Bible study resources. In each of the cities and churches I've worked in foreign and domestic missions contexts, I have sought out such solid resources and Bible study materials for women's small groups. None of the books or studies I came across seemed to address some of the issues I know women of all ages face, or if the materials did, it was not in such a way as to facilitate small group discussion and encourage leadership amongst all the women.

While I noticed this void in English women's Bible study materials, the chasm in Spanish, my second language, was even greater. So, over the years, I have, with the help of other women, written Bible studies in both languages and designed curriculums for women's small groups. These studies have been simple enough for anyone to lead and deep enough for everyone to grow.

With no desire of glory for myself, I realized that it would be selfish of me and of whatever local ministry in which I served to hold onto these resources and Bible study materials. God was calling me to share them on a much more global level.

So, as Isaiah said in one of my favorite verses, "Here am I, send me!" (Isaiah 6:8)

My response to this calling came with a clear vision of what God wanted me to do and how He wanted me to challenge and connect with other women through the image of an *Iron Rose Sister* – a Christian sister who can serve like iron sharpening iron (Prov. 27:17) while encouraging and inspiring each other to be as beautiful as a rose in spite of a few thorns.

The *Iron Rose Sister Ministries* structure provides a format for approaching these small group Bible studies and also facilitates a network of Christian sisters across the Americas. *Human AND Holy* is the first of many other small group women's Bible studies and other resources that will be provided through this new bilingual ministry.

While a part of me wants to write and share my own opinions, interpretations, experiences, etc., I realize that it is not how we learn. We learn what we've learned after having wrestled over it, discussed it with others, learned from others, prayed, and grown with others.

If you have had the opportunity to participate in a good women's Bible study group, you understand what I can't begin to explain: the growth and blessing of discussing and praying together with other women! We serve a living and active God and He is at work when we come together and invite Him to lead! If you haven't had such an opportunity in the past, I'm excited to show you a whole new world of growth and potential through the *Iron Rose Sister Ministries* small group Bible studies.

The goal of these studies is to be presented in such a way that provides you and your group of *Iron Rose Sisters* with the opportunity to allow the Holy Spirit to shape and mold each of us in partnership with each other. I wouldn't want to force-feed you my own interpretation, but rather provide you with the tools for growth. Nor would I want to spoon-feed you as a mother bird who has already chewed it up for her babies. I believe in each of you and your desire to grow as a daughter of the King, a beautiful rose that God is pruning and watering to create a beautiful bouquet in His kingdom!

Inasmuch as I firmly believe that *Iron Rose Sister Ministries* is what God has called me to, I trust that He will equip and strengthen each of us with all we need to work toward that vision. Thank you for your prayers toward that end and please spread the word to other women who long to be a part of this vision!

For more information or to book an *Iron Rose Sister Ministries* seminar in your area, please visit *www.IronRoseSister.com* or contact Michelle directly at ironrosesister@gmail.com

Iron Rose Sister Ministries
BIBLE STUDIES FORMAT

The *Iron Rose Sister Ministries (IRSM)* Bible Studies are designed for a small group context. Even if it were possible for me to give you "all the answers" and share my perspective on the verses and concepts being presented, I cannot emphasize enough the value of fellowship, discussion and prayer with other Christian sisters! The format of the *IRSM* Bible Studies allows for greater discussion, depth of insight and unique perspectives. If you don't follow the book exactly, that's okay! I invite you to make the studies your own, to allow the Spirit to lead, and to treat the studies as a guide and a resource, not a formula.

The *IRSM* Bible Studies also provide the opportunity for spiritual journaling on a personal level. I encourage you to date the chapters and add notes in the margins in addition to answering the questions. The 'Common Threads' will also allow you to chronicle your personal growth individually and in communion with your *Iron Rose Sisters*.

Common Threads in IRSM Studies

an area in which you are striving to grow and bloom

a thorn you are working on removing

an area in which you are striving to dig deeper or need to have someone hold you accountable

Using the image of the rose and the *IRSM* logo, the bloom of the rose represents areas we come to recognize in which we long to grow. Through these studies, we can also identify thorns we'd like to work on removing or need help to remove. They may be thorns like Paul's (II Corinthians 12:7-10), but by identifying them, we can know where they are and either dull them or stop sticking ourselves and others with them. The final Common Thread is the iron which is best defined and facilitated in communion with other Christian sisters, *Iron Rose Sisters*.

What is an *Iron Rose Sister*?

An *Iron Rose Sister* is a Christian sister who serves as iron sharpening iron (Prov. 27:17), encouraging and inspiring others to be as beautiful as a rose in spite of a few thorns.

Purposes of *Iron Rose Sister* Relationships:

- Encouragement and inspiration
- Prayer
- Understanding and affirmation
- Confidentiality
- Spiritual audit (*IRS*)
- Mutual call to holy living
- Spiritual friendship and conversation

Recommendations for *Iron Rose Sister Ministries* Bible Studies:

- Allow for at least an hour and a half meeting time weekly.
  o We're women – we like to talk!
  o Prayer time
  o Depth of conversation and discussion
- Rotate the leading of the discussion among EACH of the women.
  o Everyone can lead!
  o Everyone will grow!
  o For additional suggestions, see the Leader's Guide (pg. 91)

- Commit to reading the chapter ahead of time.
  - o The discussion will be richer and deeper if everyone comes prepared.
  - o How much you put in will be directly proportional to how much you get out.
  - o You will need to do these studies with your favorite Bible in hand.
  - o All verses, unless otherwise noted, are quoted from the New International Version.
- Follow up with each other during the week.
  - o Prayer
  - o Encouragement
  - o 'Common Threads'

The *IRSM* logo designation is used to highlight questions that lend themselves to good group discussion: ice-breakers, questions for depth of insight or additional perspectives, and areas for growth and sharing.

INTRODUCTION

Think of the last time you read or heard a story that pulled at your heart or that you identified with profoundly. The stories we most connect with are those that express a depth of human emotion. Even if we haven't shared the exact experience, we join with the person on their journey through their expression of the human condition – whether it is an expression of pain, sorrow, anger, or joy... I invite you, through this study series, to connect with Jesus and connect with one another on a journey of human emotion and the human condition.

As women, we experience emotions and life situations differently than men and it is my prayer that we can explore together a holy way of handling those emotions and experiences, following the example of Christ as He walked on this earth.

It can be easy to dismiss the human nature of Jesus or only focus on certain aspects of it out of fear of disrespecting His deity. I propose that we look at Jesus as Human AND Holy – called out as a human to live in a holy way, according to human nature, but not according to the sinful nature. There is a difference. And we'll explore that difference through various emotions and situations that Jesus faced, leaving us an example as we, too face those emotions and struggles on a daily basis.

Satan wants to capitalize on the guilt or frustration that comes from our imperfections. Do you ever get frustrated that you're not the Superwoman described in Proverbs 31? I certainly need more sleep than that woman must get! Through Jesus' example, we can give ourselves permission to be human while striving to be holy. There's a freedom that comes from understanding that distinction between human nature and sinful nature – not a freedom to sin (Romans 6:1), but a freedom to be all that God calls us to be as Human AND Holy.

Please join me and your other *Iron Rose Sisters* on this journey.

CHAPTER I

WHAT DOES IT MEAN TO BE HUMAN AND HOLY?

We're all quirky or nerdy in one way or another. I, for example, am a horrible klutz. It's quite entertaining to some, but not as much fun for me when I find all the bruises, bumps or scrapes that I don't remember getting.

Name one of your most interesting or humorous qualities. Okay, you don't have to limit it to just one ;)

Do you think Jesus had any of those qualities?

Whether from funny ways you might imagine from Jesus' childhood or observable ways during His ministry, how can we see the humanity of Jesus?

Using specific examples from Scripture, in what ways was Jesus human?

What about when He had His parents worried when they thought they had lost Him at age 12 (Luke 2:41-52)? What about when He cried at Lazarus' death (John 11:35)?

Is it hard to think of Jesus as human? Why or why not?

What are the top 3 things that make *us* human (besides being born)?

One thing that distinguishes humans from animals is our ability to sin.

We see in Hebrews 4:15, that "… we have one who has been tempted in every way, just as we are – yet he did not sin." Is it true temptation if you lack the ability to sin?

For example, after 40 days of fasting and praying in the desert (Luke 4:1-13), how was Jesus tempted and how *could* He have sinned?

So, was Jesus *capable* of sin?

Yes, that's a loaded question – one that will take some wrestling over and chewing on. As Emmanuel, "God with us," was Jesus able to sin? As the son of Mary and recognized son of Joseph, being 100% human while He was 100% God, was it possible for Jesus to sin?

These can be challenging concepts to wrap our heads around and I hope you are able to discuss this further with your *Iron Rose Sisters*. Jesus was God in human form. John 1:14 affirms that "the Word became flesh and made his dwelling among us." He was sent to earth for a purpose. One such purpose was to be a high priest in the order of Melchizedek (not of the tribe of Levi).

Such a high priest truly meets our need – one who is holy, blameless, pure, set apart from sinners, exalted above the heavens. Unlike the other high priests, he does not need to offer sacrifices day after day, first for his own sins, and then for the sins of the people. He sacrificed for their sins once for all when he offered himself. For the law appoints as high priests men in all their weakness; but the oath, which came after the law, appointed the Son who has been made perfect forever. – Hebrews 7:26-28

In what ways was Jesus holy?

Do we ever see Jesus' humanity and His holiness in conflict? His time in the Garden of Gethsemane is probably the most obvious example (Matthew 26:36-46), but can you think of any others?

Do you ever feel like *your* humanity and holiness are in conflict?

3

Yes, I realize that's probably a rhetorical question, but is it of comfort to realize that not only do we feel our humanity and holiness in conflict, but that Jesus did too?

❧ In what ways have you felt your humanity and holiness in conflict?

Or, at times, do you feel so sinful or distant from God that it is hard to even allow yourself to be called holy?

It is common to feel unworthy of being called holy or to fear having a "holier than thou" attitude. What does Hebrews 2:11 say in response to this? "Both the one who makes people holy and those who are made holy are of the same family. So Jesus is not ashamed to call them brothers and sisters."

We are called to be holy just as He who called us is holy. How would you explain holiness to someone?

Read 1 Peter 1:13 – 2:3 and list at least 5 descriptions or characteristics of holiness.

_____

_____

_____

_____

_____

Recap some of the characteristics of holiness as found in I Peter 1:13 – 2:3

Does perfection come into that list?   Does holiness = perfection?

Let's clarify and be certain of what holiness is. What is the definition of holiness?

According to the *New International Version Study Bible* (1995, Zondervan), "to be holy is to be set apart – set apart from sin and impurity, and set apart to God."

Holy = set apart

Holy ≠ perfection

This is one of the biggest areas in which Satan takes advantage. He affirms that we should be like Jesus, He who knew no sin (II Corinthians 5:21, I Peter 2:22), but twists the truth by leaving out any reference to grace and distorting God's true call to holiness as "set apart." In Satan's deception, he has us convinced of the lie that we need to be like Jesus was, 100% God in the flesh – the perfect Superhuman without sin. Yes, Jesus was perfect, blameless, without sin. He was 100% God, but He was also 100% human. *Human AND Holy.* Set apart for God.

We will always fall short in our own efforts to be 100% perfect like God, as Romans 3:23 affirms: "For all have sinned and fall short of the glory of God." We cannot do it alone and it may seem like a hopeless venture. However, we *can* follow Jesus' example as wholly and holy human – someone who walked on this earth, set apart for God's purpose, no matter what the human condition He faced.

Thankfully, when we lose the battle to be holy in those human situations, when we fall short and sin, God has given us a message of hope and not of condemnation. "But now that you have been set free from sin and have become slaves of God, the benefit you reap leads to _____, and the result is _____." (Romans 6:22)

Again, before we get too overwhelmed by our lack of holiness or our inability to achieve perfection, we can be encouraged by Jude 24-25. "To him who is able to keep you from stumbling and to present you before his glorious presence without fault and with great joy – to the only God our Savior be glory, majesty, power and authority, through Jesus Christ our Lord, before all ages, both now and forevermore! Amen." May we claim and own this promise!

Therefore, since holiness is not about us attaining perfection here on earth of our own efforts, but about being "set apart" in a process of transformation (sanctification)…

How do you interpret "set apart" in your own life? What are we set apart *from*? What are we set apart *for*? What Bible verses help answer that question?

Since Jesus' holiness is not about His perfection, what was Jesus set apart *from*? What was He set apart *for*? Where do we see this spoken of in Scripture?

How did the ways in which Jesus was set apart affect His humanity?

As Christians, we aren't perfect. We're wholly and holy humans. Just like Jesus.

Over the course of this study, we will be exploring what it means to be Human AND Holy, like Jesus; how to be in the world, but not of the world. Jesus had anger, felt betrayed, was sad, frustrated, stressed and even overwhelmed. Yet He knew no sin. Mind. Blown.

You may be wrestling over these concepts and feel you don't have the "right answer" to the questions presented in the chapter. There are no "right or wrong" answers (except what directly contradicts Scripture). The purpose of these studies is not to arrive at a perfectly correct, scripted answer on your own. Remember, the purpose is to wrestle over these concepts in community with your other *Iron Rose Sisters* and gain new insight and depth of understanding through the exploration of Jesus as Human AND Holy in the Bible. Through this process, we will be able to better discern how we can follow His example of holiness while encouraging and challenging each other along the path of our human lives.

Spend some time together sharing and praying over your first answers to the Common Thread elements (described fully in *IRSM* Bible Studies Format, page xv).

What do you hope to gain from this *IRSM* Bible Study with your new *Iron Rose Sisters*? Or how would you like to grow spiritually? Is there something to which God is already calling you?

How you'd like to grow and bloom _____

_____

A thorn you'd like to remove _____

_____

An area in which you'd like to dig deeper or need someone to hold you accountable

_____

_____

A message of hope, an encouraging word, or Scripture

_____

_____

CHAPTER 2

THE HOLY SPIRIT

🌹 Fill in the blank with a one or two-word description of God that is most comforting to you or encapsulates one of His promises (example below):

God is _____.

God is *not* _____.

I know that God is _____ because _____

_____

I trust that God is _____ even when _____

_____

Example:

God is <u>a loving Father.</u>

God is *not* <u>condemning.</u>

I know that God is <u>faithful</u> because <u>I see how He walks with me through the good times and the bad – never leaving me nor forsaking me.</u>

I trust that God is <u>in control</u> even when <u>I feel confused and my world appears to be spinning out of control.</u>

🌹 Refreshing our memory from last week:

I know that Jesus is *human* because _____

_____.

I know that Jesus is *holy* because _____

_____.

How can I know if I am holy? What makes me holy?

Read the following verses as they respond to these two questions:

How can I know if I am holy? What makes me holy?

Hebrews 2:11

Hebrews 10:9-14

I Corinthians 1:2

Ephesians 1:3-14

II Timothy 1:9-14

There are some special promises and comforting verses in the above passages. God CHOSE us to be holy! He considers us as a part of His family!

Based on the verses listed above, explain the relationship between holiness and the Holy Spirit.

Check out these verses about the Holy Spirit.

John 14:26

Acts 1:2, 8

Acts 2:38

Acts 5:32

In your opinion, which of these verses is most key for understanding the Holy Spirit in the context of Human AND Holy?

Does having the Holy Spirit make me more holy?

Now let's see if we have the emPHAsis on the same syllABle. How did you read that question: Does having the Holy Spirit make me more holy?

Does having the Holy Spirit **make** me more holy?
Does having the Holy Spirit make **me** more holy?
Does having the Holy Spirit make me **more** holy?

Discuss together as a group the three different ways to ask and answer the question: Does the Holy Spirit make me more holy? What Scriptures support your answers?

Thanks be to God, we are not in this Human AND Holy struggle alone! God has given us the promise of the Holy Spirit and His power to walk with us on this journey of transformation – a process we cannot handle nor a holiness we can obtain on our own. He has given us the example of His Son while He walked on this earth, and He has provided us with the support of our fellow sisters in Christ, our *Iron Rose Sisters*, as we join on this journey together.

Read Ephesians 3:14-21 and count how many times the word "power" is used. How many times? _____ What a promise!

Which verse in Ephesians 3 fills you with power or hope in this journey of transformation toward holiness?

Reflection: What aspect of your humanity do you long for the Holy Spirit to help make more holy? You may see it as a weakness, but it is something God can use powerfully in His kingdom! Remember. Holy = set apart; holy ≠perfect.

What example of Jesus can lead you through that struggle?
List a verse that demonstrates His teaching on that subject or a verse that shows Him facing a similar Human AND Holy battle.

Is there an aspect of the character of God that can bless you in that journey?

Identify a Scripture that speaks to that specific promise of God.

How can the Holy Spirit guide you in your journey toward holiness? What is a verse that describes the Spirit's power in our lives for transformation?

The Reflection Question (above) leads directly into the Common Thread elements. Be prepared to share any new areas in which you'd like to have the support and prayers of your *Iron Rose Sisters*. If the Common Threads or your responses to them seem awkward at this point, don't dismay. There are some chapters in which the Common Threads will come more naturally and others that may require more prayer or thought.

Before writing your Common Threads this week, let's look back at the purposes of the *Iron Rose Sister* Relationships, especially as they pertain to the Common Threads.

What is an *Iron Rose Sister*?

An *Iron Rose Sister* is a Christian sister who serves as iron sharpening iron (Prov. 27:17), encouraging and inspiring others to be as beautiful as a rose in spite of a few thorns.

Purposes of *Iron Rose Sister* Relationships:

- Encouragement and inspiration
- Prayer
- Understanding and affirmation
- Confidentiality
- Spiritual audit (*IRS*)
- Mutual call to holy living
- Spiritual friendship and conversation

Regarding an aspect of your humanity you long to make more holy…

How would you like to grow and bloom?

_____

_____

What is a thorn you'd like to remove?

_____

_____

Identify an area in which you'd like to dig deeper or need someone to hold you accountable.

_____

_____

Make note of a message of hope, an encouraging word, or Scripture.

_____

_____

Human AND Holy. That's our struggle. We strive to be holy without neglecting the human side. Are we doomed because we are subject to the failings and temptation of the flesh? Stay tuned for more examples, lessons, and hope in that journey!

CHAPTER 3

HUMAN NATURE VS. SINFUL NATURE

I grew up in a Christian home and through the teaching of my parents and the teaching of the church, fueled by my oldest-child need to perform to perfection, I became overwhelmed by the pressure to avoid any and all sin. Sin was wrong. Sin was bad. Sin made you a horrible person. But sin was unavoidable.

Sin still is all of those things. But thanks be to God, we have an amazing promise in Romans 8:1. "Therefore, there is now no condemnation for those who are in Christ Jesus." What a blessing and a freeing promise!

However, the rest of that chapter, for me, has lent itself to some confusion.

Read Romans 8:1-17.

These verses are Paul's answer to what I call the tongue-twister passage (Romans 7:14-28) – the human dilemma of doing what we don't want to do and not doing what we want to do. So if the solution, explained in chapter 8, is that we are to live according to the Spirit and not according to the flesh, how do I handle the aspects of my human / fleshly nature that aren't sinful?

Or is it all sinful and I can't give myself permission to be human?

✤ Does the mere fact that I'm human and have a fleshly nature become my automatic condemnation? Why or why not?

✤ If that were the case, wouldn't that then be an automatic condemnation of the Messiah when He came in the flesh? How so or how not?

Maybe you've never thought through this apparent contradiction or wrestled with performance-based Christianity. I have. And when faced with the intensity of human emotions that stemmed from difficult life events, I wrestled harder over this concept and through my struggle, gained permission and an example, through Christ Himself, to be human. Not sinful. Just human.

You may already have all of this figured out, but join me on this journey to clarify what I believe is a vital distinction.

✤ How would you distinguish between our human / fleshly nature and our sinful nature? Or is there a difference?

Which is Romans 8 referring to?

Why is there so much confusion on this point?

Let's look at Romans 8:8 in three different versions of the Bible:[1]

> "Those who are in the realm of the flesh cannot please God." (New International Version, 2011)

> "So, then, those who are in the flesh cannot please God." (New King James Version)

> "Those people who are ruled by their sinful selves cannot please God." (New Century Version)

What did you notice? Did any light bulbs go off? (Feel free to look at additional versions.)

Let's read Romans 8:1-8 in the New Century Version and see what we can glean from that translation.

> So now, those who are in Christ Jesus are not judged guilty. Through Christ Jesus the law of the Spirit that brings life made you free from the law that brings sin and death. The law was without power, because the law was made weak by our sinful selves. But God did what the law could not do. He sent his own Son to earth with the same human life that others use for sin. By sending his Son to be an offering for sin, God used a human life to destroy sin. He did this so that we could be the kind of people the law correctly wants us to be. Now we do not live following our sinful selves, but we live following the Spirit.

> Those who live following their sinful selves think only about things that their sinful selves want. But those who

---

1 I am not advocating any specific version of the Bible over another, but do encourage the study of multiple versions for a broader and deeper understanding of Scripture.

live following the Spirit are thinking about the things the Spirit wants them to do. If people's thinking is controlled by the sinful self, there is death. But if their thinking is controlled by the Spirit, there is life and peace. When people's thinking is controlled by the sinful self, they are against God, because they refuse to obey God's law and really are not even able to obey God's law. Those people who are ruled by their sinful selves cannot please God.

As believers in Christ, we all share a desire to live by the Spirit, to have our thinking controlled by the Spirit, and to benefit from the life and peace that come from that kind of Spirit-living. The big question is: how do we accomplish that while still being subject to our human nature?

Jesus led the way in human nature so that we might have hope.

"Since the children, as he calls them, are people of flesh and blood, Jesus himself became like them and shared their human nature. He did this so that through his death he might destroy the Devil, who has the power over death." (Hebrews 2:14, Good News Translation)

Throughout the following ten weeks, we will look at Jesus' example of how He submitted His human nature to the Spirit's lead and trusted His Father in total surrender.

"To this you were called, because Christ suffered for you, leaving you an example, that you should follow in his steps. 'He committed no sin, and no deceit was found in his mouth.' When they hurled insults at him, he did not retaliate; when he suffered, he made no threats. Instead, he entrusted himself to him who judges justly." (I Peter 2:21-23, NIV)

We see, even in the verses in I Peter, some examples of common human situations that Jesus faced. These were situations that would've tested His ability to not allow His human nature to lead him down a sinful path as

Peter did when Jesus predicted His own death. "Jesus turned around and said to Peter, 'Get away from me, Satan! You are an obstacle in my way, because these thoughts of yours don't come from God, but from human nature.'" (Matthew 16:23, GNT)

Using the example of Peter in Matthew 16:21-28, what is the difference between sinful nature and human nature?

How would you explain Jesus' reaction to Peter? Was it wrong for Peter to want to protect his friend? Why or why not?

Is there a way to discern that difference between human and sinful nature? Where do we start?

"So, my brothers and sisters, we must not be ruled by our sinful selves or live the way our sinful selves want. If you use your lives to do the wrong things your sinful selves want, you will die spiritually. But if you use the Spirit's help to stop doing the wrong things you do with your body, you will have true life. The true children of God are those who let God's Spirit lead them." Romans 8:12-14 (NCV)

In what aspect of your human nature do you need to walk more closely with the Spirit, allowing Him to lead?

❀ An area in which you'd like to grow and bloom _____

_____

⟞⟞⟞⟞ A thorn you'd like to remove _____

_____

| An area in which you'd like to dig deeper or need someone to hold you accountable

_____

_____

A message of hope, an encouraging word, or Scripture

_____

_____

I pray that the clarification of the distinction between human nature and sinful nature presented in this chapter brings hope and promise in your personal struggle to be Human AND Holy. In subsequent weeks, we will have the opportunity to explore these concepts as they specifically relate to various aspects of our human nature; and we will follow Jesus' example through each of those contexts.

CHAPTER 4

BROKENNESS, PAIN, AND LOSS

We will start this chapter with an article I wrote for the *New Wineskins* magazine May 2013 edition.

Broken in God's Right Hand

Have you ever been in a place of pain where you could only take life a moment at a time, maybe an hour at a time, prayerful that you would get to a place of taking a day at a time as so many recommended? I've been there. Recently. Deeply and profoundly. But God is faithful and I am at a place now where I can share at least a small part of my story.

No matter what the source of our pain or the context of our hurt, there is a raw place of human emotion that is so overwhelming and so vast it can leave you feeling disconnected from yourself. You are unable to think, to move, to breathe, or function. The emotions are so present, so intense that there is no room in your brain or your being to process anything else – not a thought, or a prayer, or a sound.

In sharing my story, I ask you not to focus on the details of the events surrounding my pain, but instead to reflect on the reality of the human condition and raw emotion that stem from those deep places of hurt that we all have and long for God to heal. I heard a great quote along the way, "Time doesn't heal all wounds. Time reveals how God heals all wounds." May His healing in my life bring about the hope of healing in yours as well.

> Praise be to the God and Father of our Lord Jesus Christ, the Father of compassion and the God of all comfort, who comforts us in all our troubles, so that we can comfort those in any trouble with the comfort we ourselves receive from God. ~ II Corinthians 1:3-4

The best part about healing is that God meets us where we are and is okay with finding us wherever we are on our journey. There have been moments where I wasn't able to pray, wasn't able to talk; when I felt so alone and dark that no one could penetrate through my shell of self-protection. For me, the shutting down and shell of self-protection came as a result of the unexpected shock and pain of my fiancé calling off our wedding and ending our relationship two and a half months before the wedding.

One morning, two days after that fateful evening, my dad came to my bedside in support and to say a prayer. He had suffered his own recent loss and pain and was hurting with me while still in his own process of healing. As he prayed over me, I was unable to process his words to God on my behalf. I began to physically shake, to emotionally overload, and mentally break-down. I couldn't handle the prayer. I wanted to know he was praying. I wanted to know others were praying. But I was not in a place to be able to physically hear those prayers.

As he finished his heartfelt words lifted to the Father, it was all I could do to not lash out at him, at God, at anything in an attempt to make the pain go away. Instead, from a strength I didn't know I had, I told him "Please know I'm not rejecting you. I'm not rejecting God. I want to know you're praying. I appreciate you're praying. But I cannot hear those prayers. I just can't. I'm sorry. I... I..." No more words would come. Even the physical pain at that point was too much. My body was shaking. My voice was shaking. I had nothing left.

A month or so later, as I reflected on that encounter and my apparent rejection of prayer, I realized several important things. God knows my heart. He knows my pain. He knew that my rejection of my dad's prayer, at that time, was not a rejection of God or of the loving support of family. And God was okay with that too! He was there, meeting me right where I was!

God promises to "never leave us nor forsake us" (Joshua 1:5). So why would He forsake me in a place of pain just because I can't put my prayers into words or process the prayers of others? Enter Holy Spirit! What a blessing that we have a Comforter that can interpret groans we cannot express.

> In the same way, the Spirit helps us in our weakness. We do not know what we ought to pray for, but the Spirit himself intercedes for us through wordless groans. And he who searches our hearts knows the mind of the Spirit, because the Spirit intercedes for God's people in accordance with the will of God. ~ Romans 8:26-27

Not only does God promise to not leave us nor forsake us in Joshua 1:5, but He promises to be with us in Isaiah 41:10, then paints a picture of embrace through verses 10 and 13. Just three weeks after the breakup, at a ladies retreat I would've preferred to skip, I was meditating on Isaiah 41. I noticed the promise in verse 10 that God "will uphold you in [His] righteous right hand." In verse 13, God takes hold of *"your* right hand and says to you, Do not fear; I will help you." His right hand with your right hand. You have to be facing each other for both parties to engage their right hands. What a realization: God, facing me, seeing my pain, taking my hand and holding me in His embrace. Wow. The God of all comfort bathed me with comfort in His loving presence at that moment, meeting me where I was and leading me toward healing.

My process of healing is not over. I thank God for providing many friends and family who have faithfully walked with me and prayed for me in my journey. And as that journey continues, I trust and share with newfound hope that I am honored to serve a loving God that never leaves us or forsakes us, even in our deepest moments of pain, loss and sorrow. May you come to know Him in that way as well. May you invite Him to meet you where you are – even if you don't have the words to voice that invitation.

****

Spend several minutes in prayer and reflection before continuing. This is a great opportunity to journal your thoughts and prayers. You can do this in the blank Notes pages at the end of the book, or in a notebook you keep separately if you are in need of additional space.

When is a time when *you* have felt broken, deep pain, or loss? Are you facing such a time right now? (Remember, this is a safe place with your *Iron Rose Sisters*.)

In what ways has God's presence been made known to you through those times? Make note of a specific verse that has held great promise for you through the pain.

You may be barely clinging to God by your fingernails, as I was, but I encourage you to hold on, to cling to Him, to trust His provision and His presence. You are not alone. There are others of your *Iron Rose Sisters* who have faced similar pain, even if the source is different. May we also be comforted by realizing that Jesus, too, faced brokenness, deep pain and loss.

When was a time when Jesus felt broken, deep pain or loss? When you look for verses or examples, be specific about the emotions Jesus expressed and the context / cause of His pain.

❧ And how did He react at those times?

Let's read these two examples and discuss how Jesus handled Himself (Human AND Holy).

John 11:1-44

Matthew 26:36-46 & Luke 22:39-46

❧ What can we learn from how Jesus reacted in holy ways to these intense human emotions in the above examples?

As it relates to a recent situation of brokenness, pain or loss in your own life, let's look at the Common Threads through which God can bring hope and healing.

How you'd like to grow and bloom through your brokenness, pain or loss

_____

_____

A thorn that's hindering that growth or healing

_____

_____

An area in which you'd like to dig deeper or need someone to hold you accountable or maybe encourage you wherever you find yourself in the healing process

_____

_____

A message of hope, an encouraging word, or Scripture

_____

_____

CHAPTER 5

RELATIONSHIPS

Take a moment to think about the people with whom you spend a lot of time. Write the names of your best friends.

When you first met, did you think you'd be the friends you are today? Why or why not? Funny stories are welcome!

Now let's narrow it down and refer only to the Christian brothers and sisters you're close to... Did you ever imagine you'd have the friendship you have with some of them today? Why or why not?

What has bonded you? What has brought you together? Common interests or opposites attract? Shared experiences or a wrong first impression? Jot down a few special memories that define these friendships and be prepared to share the joy and blessing of those relationships.

Growing up, mom used to say that her four daughters made a bouquet. Our hair was dark brown, medium brown, red, and light brown. Our heights range from 5'2" to 5'10". You may or may not be able to pick us out of a crowd and know we are sisters, but we most certainly are; with bonds formed over Barbie dolls, playing store and church, pulling each other's hair and even inflicting a few scars (sorry!). Over the years, there have been things that have brought us together and others that have temporarily torn us apart. Through it all, as my youngest sister, Chrystal, said one day, "We're sisters. I know you without you having to explain. We'll be there for each other and put up with one another even when we don't want to, because we're family."

You may not have been blessed, as I have been, to share in the unique bond of sisterhood in your immediate family, but the sentiment expressed by my youngest sister is the type of depth and commitment that I also have known in relationship with my Christian brothers and sisters and one that I pray you, too, can experience with brothers and sisters in Christ. And while my sisters by birth and I are each very unique, some of my closest friends and I may not be the most likely selection of who you would pick out of a crowd to be close friends either.

I would consider myself the traditional, classic, red rose. It's my favorite. But amongst some of my closest friends, there's a blinged-out pink rose, an anything-but-pink rose, a leopard print rose, a flowering carpet rose (incredibly robust: winter hardy, disease and pest resistant as well as free flowering), a peace rose, a white rose and many others... What kind of rose would you describe yourself to be? How about your *Iron Rose Sisters* or other friends? Feel free to draw a bouquet representing your *IRSM* group.

❀ When with your *IRSM* group, share what type of rose you describe yourself as and the types of roses you think each other might be. You can also share your bouquet. (No judging, artists!)

❀ What about Jesus and the 12 apostles? Would you have ever selected that band of brothers to join together for three years? Why or why not?

Name as many of the 12 apostles and their professions as you can, from memory. Then fill in the other names and professions using the following references: Luke 6:12-16 & 5:1-11, 27-28, Matthew 4:18-22 & 9:9-13, Mark 1:16-20 & 3:13-19.

Who do you think were the most likely to get along? The least likely? What do we know about their personalities?

Was there ever jealousy among the apostles? (Mark 10:35-45)

List the men that were in Jesus' inner circle. (Mark 14:32-42)

❀ What did Jesus ask those three guys to do for Him in Mark 14? Why?

❀ Considering the human side of Jesus, how would you describe the kind of relationship He had with the apostles? Was it one-sided or were they friends? Can you picture Jesus saying, "Does Bartholomew have a rock in his sandal again?" or "Somebody nudge Andrew. He's snoring!"

Even though Jesus spent countless times in prayer with His Father, He also spent a lot of time developing friendships with twelve men, and deeper relationships with three of them. We were created to be in relationship – with God and with one another. From the Father, Son, and Spirit to Jesus and the twelve apostles, we see examples in Scripture of relationship. Today, with Christ as the head and as our example to follow, we form part of the body of Christ and are blessed with the relationships we can have in Christ, especially with our *Iron Rose Sisters*.

❀ Describe some specific ways in which we see Jesus' relationships with His twelve apostles as holy – set apart from the world and for God.

❀ How can we make our relationships more holy – set apart from the world and for God?

❀ How would you like to grow and bloom in your relationships?

_____

_____

What's a thorn you'd like to remove (this may be a relationship of bad influence or a spirit of gossip in a certain relationship)?

_____

_____

What's an area in which you'd like to dig deeper or need someone to hold you accountable in your relationships?

_____

_____

A message of hope, an encouraging word, or Scripture

_____

_____

CHAPTER 6

MISUNDERSTANDINGS

Just because we all speak the same language doesn't mean that we will always understand each other. Twins have been found to develop their own language and some people can spend so much time together that they will finish each other's sentences. And then there are those that say something and you wonder if they just arrived from another planet!

Translate the following phrases:

These If Hill Wore[2]
Abe Odd Hull Luck Oak[3]
Ask Rude Arrive Her[4]
Gladly the Cross-eyed Bear[5]
Just a little chocolate Jesus[6]

These are humorous examples of misspoken phrases or poorly interpreted songs (answers in the footnotes), but what about the deep frustration of being misunderstood? Have you been there? How'd you feel in those situations?

---

2   The Civil War
3   A bottle of coke
4   A screwdriver
5   Gladly, the cross I'd bear
6   Just a little talk with Jesus

My dad used to say, "It's a pity all we speak is English." He longed for a different language or a second language with which to try and express the breadth and depth of what he wanted to say. Some of that also probably had to do with men and women speaking a distinct language since he was in a house-full of girls (ha!) but this is not just a gender-based challenge.

❀ Describe a time you have felt misunderstood – not just the many examples that have to do with poor cell phone service. Include the emotional reactions and feelings that stemmed from the misunderstanding.

❀ Did you get frustrated and give up? Or did you fight determinedly to get your point across? (Additional reflection: Do we fight as determinedly to understand someone else?)

❀ When is it worth fighting to be understood? Why?

What about a time when you were fighting to stand up for what you believe and knew to be right? What made it worth fighting for?

Why do you think you were misunderstood or your message was not being heard?

What do you think would happen if Jesus felt misunderstood? Check out Matthew 13:53-58 and John 16:16-18. Describe how you think Jesus felt based on the description of His reaction in these Scriptures.

How many parables did the disciples or other followers understand immediately? _____ Yes, I know He was sometimes speaking in parables in order to hide the full meaning, but do we ever see Him getting frustrated about them just not getting it?

Read Mark 8:14-21. How did Jesus react?

Now go over to Luke 4 and read verses 16-30. What happened there?

How did they react to Jesus?

Anyone ever been furious with you like that? *Too bad we don't have the ability to just walk right through the crowd! (v. 30)* If so, what did they do to show their anger or frustration?

Was this a case of simple misunderstanding or a lack of respect? What is the difference and how does that influence our own reactions?

Which do you think would hurt worse: the crowd rejecting His message and wanting to kill Him or the disciples misunderstanding Him?

Which hurts worse for us? Friends and family misunderstanding us or strangers? Why?

The beauty of these verses shows us that Jesus understands! Starting at age 12, we see examples of Jesus being misunderstood by His parents for being about His Father's work (Luke 2:41-52). During His ministry, Jesus' family actually thought He was crazy and didn't believe His teaching (Mark 3:20-21, John 7:5)!

What a blessing to have a Savior that empathizes with us in our struggles and understands human nature!

What examples did Jesus leave us for how to respond to being misunderstood?

Matthew 13:58

Mark 8:17-21

Luke 4:30

Luke 2:49-52

Which of these four examples meant the most to you and why?

Reflection: How does pride enter into our frustrations of being misunderstood?

When you find yourself being misunderstood, how can you grow and bloom in your reactions?

_____

_____

What is the thorn in your side when being misunderstood?

_____

_____

Is there an area in which you'd like to dig deeper or need someone to hold you accountable?

_____

_____

A message of hope, an encouraging word, or Scripture

_____

_____

There are many other contexts in which we see that Jesus even more deeply misunderstood by the apostles. The most painful example of that led to Jesus being betrayed by them – another human condition we will consider in the following chapter.

CHAPTER 7

BETRAYAL

Jesus knew the pain of betrayal: the depth of pain that comes from a heart being broken by someone we know and love. I won't even ask if you've ever felt betrayed. We all have. Whether it was by the friend who promised they'd pick you to be on their team in elementary school, by a boyfriend, by family, by a spouse, or by a close friend. We know that pain and don't want to ever relive it. How should we handle it? I can't say that I've always handled it perfectly. And, unfortunately, I've been the betrayer a time or two.

This week, we'll look at betrayal and it will flow nicely into the next two week's studies: Anger and Forgiveness. Please continue to walk with me and your *Iron Rose Sisters* on this journey. You are not alone and while I know these aren't the most light-hearted topics, we will gain hope, understanding and wisdom through the exploration of these topics and Jesus' example: Human AND Holy.

As we examine the instances in which Jesus was betrayed, we'll answer the same questions for each context.

When you gather together, discuss your answers and any patterns discovered from the five contexts presented.

1. Who was/were the betrayer(s)?
2. What was Jesus' relationship with the betrayer(s)?
3. In what way was Jesus betrayed?

4. How did Jesus react?
   a. What are the *human* elements of Jesus we see through the betrayals?
   b. What are the *holy* examples of Jesus we see through the betrayals?
5. How did the betrayer(s) react after realizing the harsh reality of the betrayal (if he/they did)?

Context 1: Matthew 12:14, Luke 22:66 – 23:25, John 19:1-16

1. Who were the betrayers?_____
2. What was Jesus' relationship with the betrayers?_____

   _____

3. In what way was Jesus betrayed? _____

   _____

4. How did Jesus react? _____

   _____

   a. What are the *human* elements of Jesus we see through the betrayals? _____

      _____

   b. What are the *holy* examples of Jesus we see through the betrayals? _____

      _____

5. How did the betrayers react after realizing the harsh reality of the betrayal (if they did)? _____

   _____

Context 2: Mark 14:27-28

1. Who were the betrayers? _____
2. What was Jesus' relationship with the betrayers? _____

   _____

3. In what way was Jesus betrayed? _____

   _____

4. How did Jesus react? _____

   _____

   a. What are the *human* elements of Jesus we see through the betrayals? _____

_____

   b. What are the *holy* examples of Jesus we see through the betrayals? _____

_____

5. How did the betrayers react after realizing the harsh reality of the betrayal (if they did)? _____

_____

<u>Context 3</u>: Matthew 26:14-16, 27:1-10, Luke 22:1-6, 21-23, John 6:70-71, John 13:1-5, 18-30, John 18:1-11

1. Who was the betrayer? _____

2. What was Jesus' relationship with the betrayer? _____

_____

3. In what way was Jesus betrayed? _____

_____

4. How did Jesus react? _____

_____

   a. What are the *human* elements of Jesus we see through the betrayals? _____

_____

   b. What are the *holy* examples of Jesus we see through the betrayals? _____

_____

5. How did the betrayer react after realizing the harsh reality of the betrayal (if he did)? _____

_____

<u>Context 4</u>: Matthew 26:31-35, 69-74, Luke 22:31-34, 54-62, John 13:36-38, John 18:15-18, 25-27

1. Who was the betrayer? _____

2. What was Jesus' relationship with the betrayer? _____

_____

3. In what way was Jesus betrayed? _____

   _____

4. How did Jesus react? _____

   _____

   a. What are the *human* elements of Jesus we see through the betrayals? _____

   _____

   b. What are the *holy* examples of Jesus we see through the betrayals? _____

   _____

5. How did the betrayer react after realizing the harsh reality of the betrayal (if he did)? _____

   _____

Context 5: Matthew 27:45-46

Who did Jesus feel betrayed by here? Have you ever felt that way? If so, how did you handle the depth of that feeling of betrayal?

Reflect on a time you felt guilty because of your reaction to a betrayal. Does seeing Jesus' reactions to betrayal give you more freedom to react or make you feel worse about your reactions? Explain.

List three common human reactions to betrayal. Star the one you struggle most with.

✊ In contrast, describe a *holy* reaction to betrayal.

✊ Jesus did an amazing job of seeing the person beyond the betrayal. Let's read that again: We should see the person beyond the betrayal and see him/her with God's eyes. A great example of this is Jesus with Peter in Luke 22:31-34, when Jesus predicts Peter's denial of Christ. Jesus says in verse 32, "But I have prayed for you, Simon, that your faith may not fail. And when you have turned back, strengthen your brothers." What would have happened if Jesus hadn't seen Peter beyond the betrayal?

How should we react when we have been the one to do the betraying?

One of the worst experiences I've had with betrayal was when I was the one who did the betraying. I betrayed a confidence in good faith that I was doing it for the right reasons – for that person's own good. It was a situation in which I needed wise counsel to know how to proceed and so I shared the girl's situation with the local preacher and his wife in an effort to help her out effectively. However, I did not let the girl know that it was a situation which merited me telling someone else. She reacted very negatively, defensively, and vindictively. I was devastated. It actually sent me into one of the three deepest depressions I've faced in my life. I let myself become consumed by the guilt from my sin and betrayal.

I allowed the situation to distance me from God and from others and when I realized that I didn't even like living with myself anymore, I finally hit my knees and surrendered to my loving Father who was waiting all along to embrace me, forgive me, and give me hope. I apologized to the girl I had hurt and though it took some time, she did come to forgive me and we rebuilt a friendship that continues to this day.

Thankfully, our gracious, merciful, and loving Father wastes no time in forgiving us when we betray Him. He sees the person beyond the betrayal and calls us back, as Jesus did to Peter, to strengthen the brothers (and sisters) when we return.

In light of this chapter's verses and reflections on betrayal, make note of the following:

How you'd like to grow and bloom _____

_____

A thorn you'd like to remove _____

_____

An area in which you'd like to dig deeper or need someone to hold you accountable

_____

_____

A message of hope, an encouraging word, or Scripture

_____

_____

CHAPTER 8

ANGER

Anger. Even the word may get your blood boiling. One of your best friends betrays you. A car cuts you off while you're on your way to church. You've stubbed your toe on the end of your bed for the hundredth time. Your friends post things on Facebook that you wish were happening in your life. Someone finished off the milk and put the empty carton in the fridge just to tempt you to crave a bowl of your favorite cereal. You realize someone lied to your face and spread that lie to others. You get chewed out by your boss for something he hasn't trained you to do. You fail a test. You get a flat tire when you're already running late. Someone breaks into your house. A family member dies of cancer.

There are so many things that provoke our anger. How do you physically react when you are angry? List a few examples.

Do you think Jesus shared any of those same physical reactions? How do you think that played out for Jesus as God in the flesh?

Using passages from the Bible, describe at least two instances in which Jesus displayed His anger.

🌹 The most popular example is probably His overturning the tables in the temple. Why did He do that? What made Him so angry? (see Matt. 21:12-13 & Mark 11:15-17)

🌹 Was His anger justified? Why or why not?

What about in these other examples: Why was Jesus angry? Was His anger "justified"? Be sure to expound on your answers.

Mark 3:5

Matthew 23

Matthew 11:20-24

We're familiar with the verse "In your anger, do not sin. Do not let the sun go down while you are still angry." (Ephesians 4:26). In His anger, did Jesus sin? How so or how did He not?

What does it look like to sin because of anger?

Just five verses later, Ephesians 4:31 says to get rid of all bitterness, rage and anger... so which is it? Have it, but don't sin in it or don't have it at all?

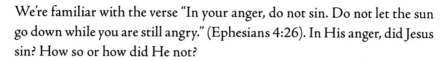 How would you explain these verses (Ephesians 4:26 & 31) to someone who's wrestling with anger?

Are there different types or sources of anger? Read James 1:19-20.

Using the scenarios mentioned earlier in the chapter and repeated below, we are going to look at three questions as they relate to healthy and unhealthy ways to deal with our anger. First, let's refresh our memories with these scenarios.

One of your best friends betrays you. A car cuts you off while you're on your way to church. You've stubbed your toe on the end of your bed for the hundredth time. Your friends post things on Facebook that you wish were happening in your life. Someone finished off the milk and put the empty carton in the fridge just to tempt you to crave a bowl of your favorite cereal. You realize someone lied to your face and spread that lie to others. You get chewed out by your boss for something he hasn't trained you to do. You fail a test. You get a flat tire when you're already running late. Someone breaks into your house. A family member dies of cancer.

What are some examples of wrong ways to handle your anger in these situations?

What would be the end result if we handled our anger in those unhealthy ways?

Using the same scenarios listed above as starting points for the discussion, how can we deal with anger and process it in a healthy way? Are there any verses or examples of Jesus that enrich our understanding of these healthy strategies?

The following is not a recommendation or endorsement of all the ideas in the list below, merely a short list of ideas and suggestions we've all heard quite often.

What do you think of the list? What has worked for you? What hasn't worked for you? Put a check by the ones that have worked for you in the past and circle any ideas you'd like to try in the future. Why did those ideas work or not work?

- ❑ Counting to 10
- ❑ Cooling down time
- ❑ Listening to music
- ❑ Seeing the situation from the other person's perspective
- ❑ Burying your face in a pillow
- ❑ Punching a pillow
- ❑ Writing an angry letter (that you don't mail)
- ❑ Avoiding the issue and/or the person
- ❑ Quoting Scripture aloud
- ❑ Setting a timer and allowing yourself to be angry for a determined amount of time
- ❑ Praying – ever tried to be angry from your knees?
- ❑ Any other good or bad ideas?

_____

_____

_____

_____

What do you consider most important about Jesus' human, yet holy responses in the following four contexts that help you know how to deal with anger?

Matthew 21:12-13 & Mark 11:15-17

Mark 3:5

Matthew 23

Matthew 21:18-22

Did Jesus address the offense or the offender? What's the difference?

When you're angry at someone, what's the best way address it with them? Are there times when it is best to not address it at all or to wait until a later time? How do we make those determinations?

What do the following verses say about how we should address our anger toward someone?

Matthew 5:21-26

Matthew 18:15-20

Personal Reflection: Dealing with the anger within ourselves is a separate issue from how we handle it with the other person. When we're angry at someone, how many times is it really a deeper, unresolved anger issue within ourselves or with someone else that we're taking out on the current person or situation?

How would you summarize the most critical issues we've discussed thus far about anger?

Before proceeding to the Common Threads, here are a few more helpful verses on anger:

Proverbs 29:11 & 22
Proverbs 15:1
Proverbs 21:14
I Corinthians 13:4-5

Thank you for wading through this tough chapter together. With this topic in particular, I encourage you to be very specific in your Common Threads. It may be best to use initials or abbreviations if you're addressing an anger issue with a certain person or situation.

How you'd like to grow and bloom _____
_____

A thorn you'd like to remove _____
_____

An area in which you'd like to dig deeper or need someone to hold you accountable
_____
_____

A message of hope, an encouraging word, or Scripture
_____
_____

CHAPTER 9

FORGIVENESS

A discussion of anger naturally leads into a look at forgiveness. Ouch. Now that's a word that cuts deep and brings up a myriad of emotions and resistance.

This chapter will help answer questions like: What is forgiveness? What is forgiveness not? What examples do we see of Jesus forgiving?

First, go through the following list and determine if the description of forgiveness is or isn't accurate, from the perspective of the one doing the forgiving.

Forgiveness for the forgiver…

is / isn't	Automatic reconciliation
is / isn't	A breaking of patterns
is / isn't	Creating a change in the other person
is / isn't	Easier said than done
is / isn't	Hard work
is / isn't	An internal process
is / isn't	A lengthy process
is / isn't	A regaining of control
is / isn't	Rationalizing or condoning an offense
is / isn't	A path to freedom
is / isn't	A sign of weakness
is / isn't	A sudden case of amnesia (forgive and forget)

What, then, does forgiveness look like? There are various stories to be told of forgiveness, but they might appear self-promoting. God is the one who deserves all the glory for the tremendous offering of complete forgiveness granted to each of His children.

But while wrestling over how to make a portion of this chapter more personal, my sister, Kim, offered to do something horrible to me so that I could forgive her and that story could be shared. She then retracted her offer stating that she wasn't sure she could do that, at least not intentionally.

And therein lies the rub. There are the cases of those who try to hurt us intentionally and the challenge of forgiving them is real and overwhelming, but we are more often faced with the challenge of forgiving those closest to us of things that were not done intentionally to harm us, but that continually cause us pain. This pain may also stem from wounds in our past, which we all have, whether from family upbringing or from difficult experiences and relationships.

Do you agree or disagree with the following quotes? Make note of any you would like to reword.

> To forgive is to set a prisoner free and discover the prisoner was you.   ~Unknown

> It is easier to forgive an enemy than to forgive a friend.   ~William Blake

> Always forgive your enemies – nothing annoys them so much.   ~Oscar Wilde

> It takes one person to forgive; it takes two people to be reunited.   ~Louis B. Smedes

> Forgiveness is accepting the pain you already know you have to live with.   ~Unknown

Forgiveness doesn't excuse their behavior. Forgiveness prevents their behavior from destroying your heart.

~Unknown

Those quotes may be profound enough for you to reflect on for the remainder of the time, but we should consider Christ's example and His teaching in Scripture as well.

In Luke 23:34, who did Jesus forgive? It may be helpful to read back through the entire chapter.

How do you think Jesus was able to forgive?!?! – as a wholly holy human. If you were put in that situation, would you have been able to forgive them? Why or why not?

Does the parable in Matthew 18:21-35 encourage you to forgive, challenge you, or aggravate you?

What do you think are the top five biggest hindrances to forgiveness?

❦ Did pride, fear, vulnerability or the longing to have things back like they were make the list?

❦ Which of these do you wrestle with the most? How do you deal with your own hindrances?

How does Jesus' example of forgiveness help with any of the aforementioned hindrances?

Since this is such a hot topic that many wrestle with, a few additional, practical suggestions have been included below that have yielded positive results in the process of forgiveness. And, yes, it is most definitely a process.

- Deep breathing exercises
- Positive thinking / attitude of gratitude
- Express yourself
  o Conflict resolution ~ non-threatening language
  o A letter of release (usually one you don't mail)
- Cultivate empathy
  o "Walk in their shoes"
- Protect yourself and move on
  o "Fool me once, shame on you. Fool me twice, shame on me."
- Get help if you need it, especially for ongoing or traumatic offenses

Forgiveness is a difficult challenge to face alone. A wisely-chosen Christian friend can walk with us as a prayer warrior and a reminder of the value of forgiveness, while avoiding a spirit of gossip, of band-wagon agreement or of affirmation of the offender as a horrible person. How can your *Iron Rose Sisters* help you in the process of forgiveness?

Prayer is a vital step toward forgiveness. As we close, take a few moments in silent prayer and reflection...

- Thanking God for His forgiveness
- Thanking God for the example of Christ's forgiveness of others while on earth
- Asking Him to help you forgive someone you're having a hard time forgiving
- And asking Him to help you forgive yourself.

How would you like to grow and bloom in the area of forgiveness? Is there anything specific you'd like to put into practice?

_____

_____

A thorn you'd like to remove _____

_____

An area in which you'd like to dig deeper or need someone to hold you accountable

_____

_____

A message of hope, an encouraging word, or Scripture

_____

_____

CHAPTER 10

ALONE TIME

I am an extrovert. I love people. I love meeting new people, especially learning about their different cultures or family traditions, and I really love spending time with family and friends. No matter what level of social butterfly you might be, we all need some time alone occasionally. Jesus understands that.

Some would describe Jesus as an extrovert; others identify more with His introverted characteristics and would describe Him as such. But alone time with God isn't about personality types. It's about communing with our Father – walking and talking with Him in such a way that guides our steps, our thoughts, our speech, our actions, our lives.

We are going to follow three of Jesus' examples in prayer and alone time with God. I encourage you to not rush through these – maybe take one day for each pattern. If you're reading this the night before you meet with your *Iron Rose Sisters* (I know, I'm a procrastinator too), take some time to do at least one of the exercises and incorporate the other two into the following week.

Prayer time also provides an excellent opportunity to journal. If you are unfamiliar with the spiritual discipline of journaling, this chapter is a great place to begin. Feel free to use a separate notebook or take advantage of the Notes pages at the end of this book. Be sure to date your entry so you can witness your own transformation, answers to prayers, etc. A basic first step is to simply write out your prayers to God – a private conversation between you and your Heavenly Father. As such, it is always at your discretion how much, if at all, you share of your journaling with anyone.

1. Jesus' Example: Alone Time with God

Matthew 14:23, Mark 6:46 – "After he had dismissed them [feeding the 5,000], he went up on a mountainside by himself to pray."

Luke 6:12 – "One of those days Jesus went out to a mountainside to pray, and spent the night praying to God."

Mark 1:35 – "Very early in the morning, while it was still dark, Jesus got up, left the house and went off to a solitary place, where he prayed."

Luke 5:16 – "But Jesus often withdrew to lonely places and prayed."

For this first exercise, I invite you to withdraw to a 'lonely place' to pray and listen to God. You may not have a mountainside nearby, but try to find a place in nature, or the highest staircase in your house or wherever you can get alone for some time with God. For young moms, this may be a challenge. For all women, be creative! Ask God to provide a specific time and place for your alone time together; He provides!

Make this time about listening – not about asking. There have been many times in my life when I don't know what to say to God. I don't have the words and the promise in Romans 8:26-27 that the Spirit will interpret my groans isn't as great an encouragement as I'd like it to be. At those times, I lean on Scripture to speak for me and to voice what I didn't even realize I wanted or needed to express.

I have included a list of verses below that are some of my favorites for meditation. You don't have to read or reflect on all of the verses listed, but choose some from this list or some of your own to mediate on. Allow God to speak to you through the verses. This is about listening, not talking. Avoid making personal requests. When your own distracted thoughts enter, answer them with Scripture.

Example: While reading Isaiah 61:10-11, your thoughts wander... and when they do, you can bring them back to a focus on your alone time with God.

> *"I greatly delight in the Lord; my soul rejoices in my God. For he has clothed me with garments of salvation and arrayed me in a robe of his righteousness..." Garments of salvation... I can't forget to transfer the laundry to the dryer before I go to bed! Oh, and call Sally Sue to remind her that we were going to go shopping together on Saturday for an outfit for... Ah! I've done it again. Father, forgive me for my wandering thoughts. I long to delight in you and rejoice in You as my thoughts become more in-tuned with your thoughts and my ways become more in-tuned with your ways. Isn't there a verse about that also in Isaiah? Yes! Chapter 55, verses 8 and 9. That definitely expresses where I am right now, "For your thoughts are not my thoughts, neither are your ways my ways,' declares the Lord."*

Possible verses for Alone Time with God:

Isaiah 61:10-11
Psalm 31
Psalm 27
Exodus 14:14
Romans 15:13
Philippians 4:19
Isaiah 41:10, 13
Psalm 139
Matthew 6:25-34
Zephaniah 3:17
Lamentations 3:22-27
Ephesians 3:14-21
Psalm 63

2. <u>Jesus' Example: The Lord's Prayer</u>

In this exercise, we will follow the pattern of the Lord's Prayer in Matthew 6:9-13, using the New English Translation. Make the Lord's Prayer your own by following the examples in *italics* below each portion of the prayer.

"So pray this way:
Our Father in heaven, may your name be honored,"
Claim three names or attributes of God by speaking them aloud

"may your kingdom come,"
Cry out to God for His church to grow and His Son to return

"may your will be done on earth as it is in heaven."
Mention a specific situation in which you long for God's will to be done, above your own will

"Give us today our daily bread,"
Thank God for His provision and ask Him to help you trust Him to meet ALL your needs according to His glorious riches in Christ Jesus (Phil. 4:19)

"and forgive us our debts, as we ourselves have forgiven our debtors."
Example: "God, you forgive us time and time again. Thank you for your example of forgiveness and please help me forgive _____. Help me see forgiveness as freedom for me and trust in You, not a condoning of any wrongdoing."

"And do not lead us into temptation, but deliver us from the evil one."
Example: "Lord, I'm so tempted to _____, even when I recognize it as Satan's trap. Please help me remember that Your way is best and replace the temptation to do something wrong with a desire and longing to do something right."

3. <u>Jesus' Example: John 17</u>

Before going to the cross, John records a lengthy prayer in which Jesus prays for Himself, for His disciples and for all believers. Read John 17 and then, following that model, make a list of things to pray over in the same three categories:

Prayers for yourself:

Prayers for the local body of believers (your local church or your *IRSM* group):

Prayers for all believers worldwide:

Be sure to pray over those areas yourself before joining with your sisters, but here's an exercise for when you gather together: On note cards or slips of paper, jot down your requests in the three categories above to pray over together as *Iron Rose Sisters*. Exchange cards and pray over each other's requests while you're gathered together and also during the following week.

Share with your *Iron Rose Sisters* some of what you experienced in your Alone Time with God.

What did you most enjoy?

Were there any verses that jumped out at you during the reading / listening? Which ones?

Did you get a sense of peace or of frustrated distraction?

How did God speak to you through your time with Him? This may not be an audible voice, but a verse that jumped out at you, a peace that overcame you, a prayer that was answered... If you journaled during that time, you may want to share something you wrote during the Alone Time with God.

Whether from something you gleaned from your Alone Time with God or a way you'd like to grow in prayer, spend some time reflecting and praying over any new Common Threads.

How you'd like to grow and bloom _____

_____

A thorn you'd like to remove _____

_____

An area in which you'd like to dig deeper or need someone to hold you accountable

_____

_____

A message of hope, an encouraging word, or Scripture

_____

_____

CHAPTER 11

HUNGRY, THIRSTY, AND INTERRUPTED

I think we're all familiar with the announcement on airplanes that goes something like this: "In case of a decrease in cabin pressure, an oxygen mask will fall. Place your mask on yourself first, before helping someone else with their mask." I always thought that strange; the instructions to perform an apparent selfish act troubled me. Thankfully, I haven't had to put those directions into action on an airplane, but I've been reminded time and time again that such instructions are not a selfish act, but rather an indication that if I don't take care of myself, I may not be adequately equipped to help take care of others.

For example, I have to be careful of my attitude and harsh words when I haven't eaten. Sometimes, I don't recognize that I need to eat until I realize that I'm getting irrationally irritable or that I'm about to crash. A friend in Venezuela was more aware of my blood sugar issues than I was. He would often encourage me to eat something in an effort to avoid my "Dr. Jekyll / Mr. Hyde syndrome," as he called it.

How can you tell when you're hungry? Thirsty? Tired?

Are you able to do what you need to do for yourself or for others when you get that way?

In this chapter, we are going to look at a few short stories of Jesus that reveal some of our most basic needs and conditions as humans – as Jesus Himself experienced them. After each of the verses below, list the basic human need, condition or situation you see Jesus facing.

Matthew 21:18 & Mark 11:12-14

Luke 10:21

John 4:4-8

John 11:33-35

Matthew 14:6-14

What's your reaction to seeing these human characteristics of Jesus? Does it make Him seem weak? How so or why not?

Whether from the above verses or others, what examples do we have of Jesus taking care of Himself (physically or spiritually) in order to be able to take care of others?

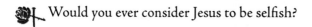 Would you ever consider Jesus to be selfish?

What about in these two stories? Mark 1:35-37 & Mark 4:35-41

What can we learn from Christ's example? Reversing the scenario, what would *we* have done in Jesus' shoes (versus what would Jesus do)?

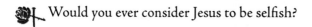 Jesus was constantly interrupted and there were many demands on His time and attention. How did Jesus balance those priorities?

What about when the little children came to Him (Matthew 19:13-15)?

One of my favorite stories in Scripture is found in Matthew 9:18-26 and is an excellent example of how Jesus handled being interrupted. How can we put His example into practice?

Jesus didn't allow His human condition to hinder holy appointments or opportunities.

What perspective did Jesus have that we can aspire to when faced with our own human limitations, emotions or weaknesses?

As an additional consideration on this concept, I'd like to share a reflection I wrote one day when I was feeling especially weak – just a few short months before launching *Iron Rose Sister Ministries*. Satan wanted to capitalize on my weakness, but I am grateful for God's strength, His promises and His answers to Satan's discouraging messages of self-doubt and confusion.

Does being an invalid make you feel invalid?

Being sick is a strange thing, especially if it's a chronic condition. I recently realized a play on words that emphasizes part of the mental and emotional battle I face when I am physically weak or sick. When I am an invalid, I feel invalid. Be sure to get the emPHAsis on the right syllABLe ;) As an INvalid, I feel inVALid. Allow me to explain:

  • You feel like a watered-down version of yourself and then a doctor doubts your description of the pain, unable to get to the root of your condition. An INvalid = inVALid?

  • Your energy and motivation are gone. You can't even remember all of what you were supposed to do anyway. An INvalid = inVALid?

  • You finally take the time to rest – recover from recent events and physically prepare for what's to come. Satan puts messages of laziness, guilt and inadequacy in your mind. An INvalid = inVALid?

+ You have discerned God's calling and long to serve as He leads, but your physical strength and ability inhibit your capacity to fulfill that calling. Doubt creeps in. An INvalid = inVALid?

+ Your physical pain accentuates and exaggerates all other negative thoughts and emotional pain. Healing on any level seems unattainable. An INvalid = inVALid?

+ Usually the one to cheer others up and be a source of strength, you have nothing left to give. An INvalid = inVALid?

+ As someone who used to take pride in her ability to multi-task, be there for others, and "do it all," you find yourself in a new place of dependence on others. An INvalid = inVALid?

+ The things that shaped your identity before are undermined or inhibited by physical limitations. An INvalid = inVALid?

Thoughts like these have pervaded my mind for the past few days and weeks. I have forced myself to recall that "greater is He that is in me than He that is in the world" (I John 4:4) and that my identity as a child of God really is enough. God is honored to call me His child and does not measure my worth by my ability to perform.

> "Therefore, in order to keep me from becoming conceited, I was given a thorn in my flesh, a messenger of Satan, to torment me. Three times I pleaded with the Lord to take it away from me. But he said to me, "My grace is sufficient for you, for my power is made perfect in weakness." Therefore I will boast all the more gladly about my weaknesses, so that Christ's power may rest on me. That is why, for Christ's sake, I delight in weaknesses, in insults, in hardships, in persecutions, in difficulties. For when I am weak, then I am strong." II Corinthians 12:7b – 10

Your Common Threads this week may be about giving yourself permission to be human! Take a moment to reflect and be encouraged through prayer in these areas.

✿ How you'd like to grow and bloom _____

_____

⸺ A thorn you'd like to remove _____

_____

| An area in which you'd like to dig deeper or need someone to hold you accountable

_____

_____

A message of hope, an encouraging word, or Scripture

_____

_____

CHAPTER 12

COMPASSION

One definition of compassion could be, "seeing someone in need and being moved and motivated into action." Growing up, I might not have been known as the most compassionate person. My sisters would say I was the bossy oldest child. My task-oriented, highly-driven nature made me not-so-sympathetic toward those who didn't meet up to my expectations. I was the hardest on myself, of course, but 'compassionate' or 'loving,' would not have been the first words someone would use to describe me. My own health issues and other difficult times in my life have made me much more compassionate, understanding, and sympathetic to others struggling or in need, which has, in turned blessed many relationships as well. For example, my relationship with my sister, Jenn, has probably grown the most through our compassionate understanding of each other and our respective health issues. I pray that I continue to grow in compassion, but at times, I still struggle with being skeptical of others in need.

Last week, my sister, Kim, described to me a child in the grocery store parking lot that was selling bracelets to raise money for his grandmother with cancer. To give or not to give? – that was the question. We all drive by people with cardboard signs at the stop light or are approached by children in parking lots.

When you see someone in need, is your first reaction to be skeptical or to be compassionate?

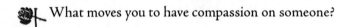 Does your reaction change depending on the circumstances? How and why?

 What moves you to have compassion on someone?

 What makes it hard for you to have compassion on someone?

Are you more like the disciples or like Jesus? (Matthew 19:13-15)

In each of the following instances, what moved Jesus to compassion?

Matthew 14:14

Matthew 15:32

Matthew 20:34

Mark 6:34

Luke 8:40-56

How did Jesus act on His compassion in these situations?

How was Jesus known for His compassion?

Would you say this was this a holy human characteristic or did this come from His God-character? Explain.

List three specific ways we show compassion to others. What does that compassion look like?

How can *we* be known for our compassion?

Do you desire to grow in your compassion or your discernment?

Matthew 10:16 is in the middle of Jesus' instructions to the disciples before He sends them out. He says, "I am sending you out like sheep among wolves. Therefore be as shrewd as snakes and as innocent as doves." How does this apply to the need for compassion?

"Finally, all of you, live in harmony with one another; be sympathetic, love as brothers, be compassionate and humble." I Peter 3:8

How you'd like to grow and bloom _____

_____

A thorn you'd like to remove _____

_____

An area in which you'd like to dig deeper or need someone to hold you accountable

_____

_____

A message of hope, an encouraging word, or Scripture

_____

_____

CHAPTER 13

TRAPPED AND IN NEED OF WISDOM

A Chinese finger trap, debates, and circular conversations... we've all felt trapped at one time or another. A friend asks an impossible question to answer. You're put on the spot and no matter what you say, you feel like you're between a rock and a hard place; no matter what you say, it will be taken wrong.

Describe a specific instance in which have you felt trapped or clueless as to how to answer in a difficult situation. How did you get out of it?

Jesus felt trapped on multiple occasions. Let's read these three examples and discuss...

1. How Jesus was trapped
2. How He responded to being trapped (quick answer, silence...)
3. How His response diffused the situation (vs. an answer that would've landed Him directly in the trap)

John 8:1-11

1. _____
_____

2. _____
_____

3. _____
_____

Matthew 22:15-22

1. _____
_____

2. _____
_____

3. _____
_____

Luke 20:1-8

1. _____
_____

2. _____
_____

3. _____
_____

Where did this wisdom come from? Was it only because He was God in the flesh?

Can we, as humans, have access to that kind of wisdom in trapped situations? How?

Let's look at one more situation in which Jesus was trapped and in need of wisdom: His temptation. The story is found in Luke 4:1-13.

We will go through this passage together and dissect each of Satan's traps and Jesus' responses. Keep in mind that the easiest lie to believe is the one that has an element of truth. The father of lies took advantage of that fact and even quoted Scripture to Jesus in his attempt to test and trap Him!

"The devil said to him, 'If you are the Son of God, tell this stone to become bread.'" (Luke 4:3) Is Jesus the Son of God? Of course! But Jesus did not respond as the devil desired because He considered the source and recognized the trap. He would've been obeying Satan and not God had He turned the stones into bread, hungry as He was after 40 days of fasting.

In verses 5-7, Satan offers to give Jesus authority and splendor if Jesus will worship him. "Jesus answered, 'It is written: 'Worship the Lord your God and serve him only.''" (Luke 4:8) Jesus knew the first and greatest command (Matthew 22:36-38) and would not do nor say anything to the contrary. He knew His Father and He knew His Father's will.

In the third test, Satan even quotes Scripture! The father of lies distorts the truth of Scripture to his own end and for his own gain. However, Jesus, yet again, considered the source and recognized the trap. He called out Satan directly and responded back with Scripture. "It is said: 'Do not put the Lord your God to the test.'" (Luke 4:12)

✜ How did Jesus do this? How was He able to recognize these temptations and resist?

What had Jesus been doing for the previous 40 days? (See also Matthew 4:1-2.)

How did that help prepare Him for Satan's traps?

✜ Do you have a story of a time the Spirit spoke for you and gave you words you didn't know you had? Be prepared to share.

Allow me to share a story… Back in the summer of 1996, a young freshman in college ventured on a mission trip to Venezuela – her first time out of the country and her first opportunity to put the Spanish she had studied in textbooks to the test. She spent the first four weeks on a campaign with about 20 other students, meeting people, inviting them to the nightly meetings conducted by the local church, studying the Bible with people and learning a lot about herself and a new culture.

After those initial four weeks, she and two other students stayed for another three weeks to follow up on all of the contacts that had been reached during the campaign. The young man that stayed spoke no Spanish and the other girl that stayed, while she was somewhat proficient, contracted salmonella and was in bed most of the remaining time.

So, this young girl, novice-level in her Spanish, and young guy, barely able to say "hola," trekked across the city, following up on dozens of people who had signed up for personal Bible studies. They would visit a home and if it was a man that had signed up for the study, Michelle, as we will call her, would translate for the young man and if it was a woman who had signed up for the study, Michelle would teach while the young man read his Bible and sipped the coffee all the students had grown to love.

On one such occasion, in the home of a lady who had signed up for a personal Bible study, Michelle was faced with a difficult question she wasn't sure of the answer to in English and felt even less equipped to answer in Spanish. She said a quick prayer and a few minutes later, realized that she had just given the most eloquent and Scriptural answer to a very difficult question. Actually, she didn't. She didn't give that answer and none of those eloquent words were her own. Even if she had been able to answer the question adequately, her Spanish was at a level that the response would have been less than eloquent.

Yes, that was me. I still remember that day vividly. I don't remember the question the lady asked, nor her name, but I will never forget the light that came on in her eyes as the Spirit took over for me and spoke through me in a way that I had never experienced before. I was hooked. I knew from that day forward that I wanted to use my life in any way possible to allow the Spirit to speak through me to shed The Light to any that wanted to hear the good news of the hope we have in Christ.

Any wisdom that we can live by or any answers we can share in trapped situations are a testimony to the power of the Spirit in the lives of those who are willing to allow Him to work. Jesus was trapped. Jesus needed wisdom. He walked with His Father and was filled with the Spirit and, therefore, was able to respond accordingly or keep silent when faced with those very human situations. The best part is that as children of God, in Christ, we have access to the same power and wisdom through the Holy Spirit as Jesus did! What a blessing in our Human AND Holy struggles!

These are the final Common Threads in our reflection of *Human AND Holy*. Spend some extra time praying over these together and feel free to look back over previous week's Common Threads as well for the prayer time with your *Iron Rose Sisters* this week.

How you'd like to grow and bloom in wisdom and attentiveness to the Spirit

_____

_____

A thorn you'd like to remove _____

_____

An area in which you'd like to dig deeper or need someone to hold you accountable

_____

_____

A message of hope, an encouraging word, or Scripture

_____

_____

CLOSING REMARKS

Thank you for your participation with me and with your *Iron Rose Sisters* in this journey of striving to be more Human AND Holy.

It is my prayer that throughout the course of this study, you have gained a greater perspective of our Lord as Human AND Holy. Not only that, but also that you have developed deep, lasting relationships with the *Iron Rose Sisters* that have walked with you on this journey. If you have completed this Bible Study series on your own, I encourage you to find a friend and share with her the way the Spirit has led and worked through you during the course of the study.

Through the Common Threads, you have recognized areas for growth, identified thorns you'd like to remove and defined areas in which you'd like to dig deeper or have someone hold you accountable. I encourage you to continue your pursuit of those Common Thread goals in the process of transformation toward Human AND Holy living. Thankfully, you are not on this journey alone. God is the author of your journey, and I pray that He will continue to carry you through in partnership with the *Iron Rose Sister* relationships you have been blessed with as well.

Stay tuned for more *Iron Rose Sister Ministries* Bible Studies to come!

For more information, check out *www.IronRoseSister.com* and sign up for the *IRSM* Newsletter by clicking on the Contact page.

REFERENCES

Bibles quoted:

THE HOLY BIBLE, NEW INTERNATIONAL VERSION®, NIV®
Copyright © 1973, 1978, 1984, 2011 by Biblica, Inc.™ Used by
permission. All rights reserved worldwide.

New International Version Study Bible (Zondervan, 1995)

Scripture taken from the New King James Version®. Copyright © 1982 by
Thomas Nelson, Inc. Used by permission. All rights reserved.

Scripture taken from the New Century Version®. Copyright © 2005 by
Thomas Nelson, Inc. Used by permission. All rights reserved.

Good News Translation® (Today's English Version, Second Edition)

Copyright © 1992 American Bible Society. All rights reserved.

NET Bible® copyright ©1996-2006 by Biblical Studies Press, L.L.C. http://
netbible.com All rights reserved.

Quotes from Chapter 9, Forgiveness

William Blake

Oscar Wilde

Louis B. Smedes

NOTES

Leader's Guide

As presented in the *Iron Rose Sister Ministries* Bible Studies Format, each *Iron Rose Sister* is encouraged to rotate leading the discussion each week.

Even if you do not feel equipped to lead or feel that you lack adequate experience to do so, it is a rich opportunity for growth and blessing. You are among sisters and friends that are supporting you in this part of your journey as well.

The following are a few tips or reminders, especially for new leaders:

- Make it your own and allow the Spirit to lead - these studies are a resource, not a script.
    - o Select which questions you would like to discuss and plan for ones you might need to skip if you are running short on time.
    - o You are welcome to add questions of your own or highlight portions of the chapter that most stood out to you, whether they were designated for discussion or not.
- Leading is about facilitating the discussion, not about having all the answers.
    - o When someone brings up a difficult situation or challenging question, you can always open it up to the group for answers from Scripture, not just personal advice.
    - o The answer may merit further study of Scripture or the consultation of someone with more experience in the Word and/or experience regarding that type of situation. And that's okay! We're digging deeper.

- Be willing to answer the designated discussion questions first and use your own examples, but avoid the temptation to do all the talking.
  - o Allow for awkward silence in order to provide the opportunity for others to share.
  - o It's okay to call on someone and encourage them to answer a specific question.
  - o "Why or why not?" are good follow-up questions for discussion.
- Include additional examples from Scripture and encourage others to do the same.
  - o Online Bible programs, such as BibleGateway.com, provide excellent resources: multiple versions of the Bible, concordances (to look up the occurrences of a word), Bible dictionaries, and commentaries.
- Give a practical wrap-up conclusion or "take-home" application from the week as you close with the Common Threads.
- Be sure to budget some time for prayer.
- Remember our purposes as *Iron Rose Sisters*, students of the Word and daughters of the King.

ABOUT THE AUTHOR

Michelle has been writing small group Bible study materials in English and in Spanish throughout her ministry career. God has led Michelle to share these resources with more women across the world through *Iron Rose Sister Ministries*. She continues to take advantage of opportunities for speaking engagements, seminars, Ladies' Days and other Women's Ministry events across the Americas, in English and in Spanish. If you would like to book a seminar in your area, please contact Michelle at ironrosesister@gmail.com or for more information, visit *www.IronRoseSister.com*

Personal Life

Michelle grew up in Baton Rouge, Louisiana, with her parents and three younger sisters. Her love and desire for helping women in their journey began early with her sisters, even when they thought she was being bossy. They've all grown a lot from those early years, but the sisterly bonds remain. Michelle has been blessed by the support of her family through all of her endeavors over the years.

Michelle enjoys time with family, cheering on the Atlanta Braves and the LSU Tigers, having coffee with friends, movies, travel and speaking Spanish. And guess what her favorite flower is? Yep. The red rose.

She currently resides in Brighton, Colorado, with one of her sisters, her brother-in-law and adorable nephew.

Ministry and Educational Experience

Michelle first felt called into ministry during her senior year at Harding University while obtaining a Bachelor of Arts degree in Communication Disorders and Spanish. She planned to join a team to plant a church in north Bogotá, Colombia, and moved to Atlanta, Georgia, after graduating in May 1999 to facilitate that church-plant. Even though the plan for a Bogotá, Colombia team fell through, Michelle continued her dream to be a part of a church-planting there, which happened in March 2000.

She worked in the Missions Ministry at the North Atlanta Church of Christ for a year and a half, before moving to Denver, Colorado, to work with English and Spanish-speaking church plantings there (Highlands Ranch Church of Christ and three Spanish-speaking congregations). During the two and a half years in Denver, Michelle continued her involvement in Bogotá, Colombia, and throughout various regions of Venezuela, visiting new church plants, teaching classes, conducting women's retreats, speaking at and assisting at youth camps, etc.

In March 2003, Michelle moved to Caracas, Venezuela, to assist with a church planting in the eastern side of the city. Her time in Caracas was focused on the East Caracas congregation, but she was also able to participate in other women's activities across the country. In the four years Michelle spent in Caracas, the congregation grew from the twelve people meeting in her apartment to almost 100 meeting in a hotel conference room. The East Caracas congregation recently celebrated its 10 year anniversary and is still going strong. A visit to Bogotá, Colombia, every three months to renew her Venezuelan visa also facilitated continued assistance with the congregation there in Bogotá.

In March 2007, Michelle transitioned back into ministry in the United States as Women's Campus Minister for the South Baton Rouge Church of Christ at their Christian Student Center facility just outside the campus of Louisiana State University. While walking with the college students there on their spiritual journey and serving in other women's ministry roles, Michelle also pursued her "nerdy passion:" Spanish. She graduated

December 2011 from Louisiana State University with a Masters in Hispanic Studies, Linguistics Concentration. Her thesis explored the influence of social and religious factors in the interpretation of Scripture.

Michelle is now following God's calling to use her bilingual ministry experience with women of all ages and cultural backgrounds to bless them with opportunities for growth and deep spiritual connection with other Christian sisters through *Iron Rose Sister Ministries.*

About *Iron Rose Sister Ministries*

Overall Mission:

A ministry that facilitates Christian sister relationships that will be like iron sharpening iron, encouraging and inspiring each other to be as beautiful as a rose in spite of a few thorns. Its goal is to provide women's Bible studies simple enough for anyone to lead and deep enough for everyone to grow. These resources will be available in English and Spanish (*Iron Rose Sister Ministries - IRSM / Ministerio Hermana Rosa de Hierro - MHRH*).

FACETS of Iron Rose Sister Ministries' vision:

F – Faithfulness – to God above all else. First and foremost: *"Seek first His kingdom and His righteousness and all these things will be added to you as well." Matthew 6:33*

A – Authenticity – We're not hypocrites, just human. *"But he said to me, "My grace is sufficient for you, for my power is made perfect in weakness." Therefore I will boast all the more gladly about my weaknesses, so that Christ's power may rest on me. That is why, for Christ's sake, I delight in weaknesses, in* *insults, in hardships, in persecutions, in difficulties. For when I am weak, then I am strong." II Corinthians 12:9-10*

C – Community – We were not created to have an isolated relationship with God. He has designed the church as a body with many parts (*I Corinthians 12*). The magnitude of "one another" passages in the New Testament affirms this design. As women, we have unique relational needs at various stages in life – whether we are going through a time in which we need, like Moses, our arms raised in support by others (*Exodus 17:12*) or are able to rejoice with those who rejoice and mourn with those who mourn (*Romans 12:15*). The *Iron Rose Sister Ministries* studies are designed to be shared in community.

E – Encouragement through Prayer and Accountability – *"As iron sharpens iron, so one person sharpens another." Proverbs 27:17* God has not left us alone in this journey.

"Confess your sins to each other and pray for each other so that you may be healed. The prayer of a righteous man is powerful and effective." James 5:16

It is our prayer that every woman that joins in this mission participates as an *Iron Rose Sister* with other women, partnering in prayer and loving accountability.

T – Testimony – We all have a "God story." By recognizing His living and active hand in our lives, we are blessed to share that message of hope with others (*John 4:39-42*). Thankfully, that story is not over! God continues to work in the transformation of lives and we long to hear your story.

S – Study – *"The Word of God is alive and active. Sharper than any double-edged sword, it penetrates even to dividing soul and spirit, joints and marrow; it judges the thoughts and attitudes of the heart." Hebrews 4:12*

In order to fully realize the blessing, benefit, and design of the *Iron Rose Sister Ministries* vision, we must go to the Creator. Through a greater knowledge of the Word, we can blossom as roses and remove a few thorns – discerning the leading of the Spirit, recognizing the voice of the Father and following the example of the Son. This is more effectively accomplished in community (small group Bible studies), but not to the exclusion of time alone with God (personal Bible study).

The structure of the *Iron Rose Sister Ministries* Bible Studies is a 12-13 week study designed to be conducted in a small group context.

Other studies to come: (in alphabetical, not anticipated production order)

Depression & Discouragement
Falling in Love with Jesus
Forgiveness
I get it! Wait… No I don't.
People are Stupid, so Why the Church?
Relationships God's Way
Scheming for God
Tough Stuff Jesus Says
Tru dat!
Where do I fit?
Wounded Warrior Princess

For more information, visit *www.IronRoseSister.com* and sign up for the *IRSM* Newsletter on the Contact page. Also, please contact us if you are interested in an *IRSM* seminar or ladies' retreat in your area. For those interested in making a tax-deductible contribution to further the work of *Iron Rose Sister Ministries*, checks can be mailed to:

Iron Rose Sister Ministries
P.O. Box 1239
Brighton, CO 80601

CPSIA information can be obtained at www.ICGtesting.com
Printed in the USA
LVOW08s2203300813

350159LV00003B/4/P